PRINCIPLES AND PRACTICES TO HELP STUDENT-ATHLETES CHAMPION CHANGE

CHAMPS U

GUIDE TO CHAMPIONING ATHLETIC TRANSITION©

By Pasha Cook
Cover photo by Tiara Marei

Copyright © 2016 by PNC Enterprises LLC. All Rights Reserved

ISBN-10: 0-9983157-0-2
ISBN-13: 978-0-9983157-0-6

All rights reserved. No part of this work may be copied, reproduced, or transmitted in any form or by any means, electronic or mechanical, including photocopying, scanning, or by any information storage or retrieval system, except as is expressly permitted under Section 107 or 108 of the 1976 United States Copyright Act, without the prior written permission of PNC Enterprises LLC. Request to the author for permission should be addressed to: info@pashacook.com

Limitation of Liability/ Disclaimer of Warranty:
While the publisher and author have used their best efforts in preparing this guide and workbook, they have no representations or warranties on the accuracy or completeness of the contents of this document.

The information published in this book represents the opinions personal research and business experience of the author. Since the success of anyone depends on upon the skill and ability of the person, the author makes no guarantees and disclaims any personal loss or liabilities that may occur as result of the use of the information contained herein.

This publication is designed to provide accurate and authoritative information regarding the subject matter covered in it. It is provided with the understanding that the publisher is not engaged in rendering legal, accounting, or other professional services. If the legal advice or another expert assistance is required, the services of a competent professional person should be sought.

Due to the ever-changing dynamic of the internet, certain website information contained in this publication may have changed. The author makes no representations about the current accuracy of the web information shared.

Table of Contents

So…What's in this Guide? 2
    My personal story of Athletic Transitioning 2
    What are the Transferable Skills of an Athlete? 2
    Mentorship Matters 4
    What was I going to do now? 5

NCAA STATS 6
    Men's Basketball 6
    Women's Basketball 7
    Football 8
    Baseball 9

SECTION 1: MY MISSION 11
    What Does CHAMPS **(U)** Stand for? 12

First things first 14
    Who are you? 14
    Who are you outside of sports? 14
    Important definitions to remember 16
    What makes student-athletes different from other students? ...16
    What's Your Plan? (Self-Assessment Questions) 18

SECTION 2: CHAMPS **(U)**-PRINCIPLES OF SUCCESS 21
    (C)-COACHABLE 22
        The Power of Mentorship 23

(H)-HUNGER FOR LEARNING 26
    Champions are always seeking to learn more 27
    Be a Student of the GAME (Research)..27
(A)-ACCOUNTABILITY 29
    Building your Accountability team 30
    Who is on your Accountability Team? 30
    Who can help me? 31

SECTION 3: (M)-MASTERING YOUR MINDSET 35
    Motivated thru mistakes..37
    Visualize your success 38
    Be Patient during the process..39

SECTION 4: (P)-PERSISTENCE 41
    So, which of the four resonated with you?...................................42
(P)-PERSISTENCE 44
(S)-DEVELOP STRENGTH THROUGH YOUR STRUGGLES 46

SECTION 5: BRAND (U) 51
Personal Branding and Social Media 53
    What's your personal brand? 53
    What are your values? 53
    GUIDE SUMMARY 58

About the Author...65
Works cited 66

CHAMPS WORKBOOK

"Looking for someone to help your student-athletes explore their hidden possibilities on and off the court? Look no further. Pasha Cook will create instant rapport and have your SAs on the edge of their seats as they discover who they are, what they want, and how to get it. It is an inspiring and transformative experience for student athletes, coaches, and administrators. I highly recommend her."

-Brian Goldstein
Director of Athletics & Recreation
LaGuardia Community College

"The Champs U guide is certainly well thought out and put together. A solid resource for student-athletes."

Leeja Carter, Ph.D.
Assistant Professor
Chair, AASP Diversity Committee
Director, Performance Excellence in Applied Kinesiology (PEAK)
Division of Athletic Training, Health, and Exercise Science (ATHES)
Long Island University-Brooklyn

"Pasha presented to the WNBA Rookies on Draft Day and offered on site support. Her knowledge, insights, and communication style is valuable and highly regarded. Additionally, Pasha has an impressive and unique combination of collegiate athletic experience and business savvy that I think makes her an excellent resource and invaluable asset to the team."

-Megan Hughes
WNBA Basketball Operations & Player Relations

"I think we should continue to have speakers that can positively influence athletes to stay motivated and think about life after athletics."

-Student-Athlete
University of Memphis

"The Champs U presentation from Pasha was everything we were looking to provide our Athlete Network interns. She was extremely engaging while providing valuable insight on the lives of student-athletes. We have received nothing but positive feedback!"

-Marti Rosche
Community Relations Director
Athlete Network

"How you respond to the challenge in the second half will determine what you become after the game, whether you are a winner or a loser."

- Lou Holtz

So…what's in this guide?

In this guide, you will learn the principles and practices that have taken me a lifetime to learn. I have worked diligently to master the art of **Intentional Transitioning**. Now, don't get me wrong, it has taken making several mistakes to finally get it right, and I am still learning and growing. However, the things I have learned will be beneficial to you as you transition and will make your road to success much easier.

My personal story of Athletic Transitioning

I started playing basketball when I was seven years old. Due to an unstable childhood environment in which I moved more than I stayed still, I eventually lost my eligibility to play the game that I loved. So, I dropped out of school in the eleventh grade.

Anywhere I could find a ball and a goal, I was there. However, when I lost my eligibility and was no longer able to play for my high school team, I lost hope of ever going to college as well. I believed, like many athletes today, that my skills and attributes of being an athlete were only great for sports and nothing else. I didn't see the bigger picture. I failed to understand that if I focused and worked hard enough, those same transferable skills that helped me become a great basketball player would later help me become a great entrepreneur, career development coach, friend, and overall a better person.

What are the Transferable Skills of an Athlete?

(Shiina et al., 2003) helps student-athletes identify skills they have learned through sports that may be applicable in career-related domains, including:

- **Communication skills** – the ability to listen, cooperate, and build relationships with others.
- **Teamwork skills** – the ability to work within a team. Companies invest a lot of money in team-building activities and training. It may sound cliché, but teamwork makes the dream work. The unity of a team can make the difference in the outcome of a project.
- **Leadership skills** – the ability to motivate and lead others.
- Ethics and proper conduct – the ability to behave responsibly, the posture to properly serve as a role model, and play or work within the rules.
- **Problem solving skills** – the ability to analyze situations, gather information and make good decisions based upon the available evidence.
- **Self-motivational skills** – the ability to self-motivate and to strive for success. This self-starting action is often needed when there is no external force or person cheering you onward.
- **Organization skills** – the ability to organize time and set effective goals.
- **Physical skills and knowledge** – the ability to stay physically fit and, at the same time acknowledge, understand and obey physical limits.
- **Coping skills** – the ability to manage emotions and cope with setbacks.
- **Execution skills** – the ability to follow instructions, stay on task and get the job done. Some refer to this as fidelity to duty.

(NCAA Innovations in Research and Practice Grant Program: https://www.ncaa.org/sites/default/files/Van%20Raalte_SA%20Career%20Development.pdf)

Mentorship Matters

Thankfully, there were people who came along and helped me to see my potential both inside and outside of sports. One of the main contributors to my success is my dear friend, mentor and former coach, Louis Ray. He has a profound passion for basketball and for helping athletes bounce back after being injured. He continues to work with NBA, NFL, WNBA, Collegiate and High School athletes, with the end-goal of helping them to get back in the **game.**

When Louis and I first met I was in my early 20's, he was forming a women's semi-pro basketball team to create a pipeline into the WNBA (Women's National Basketball Association) for former collegiate and overseas basketball players. I was so excited to have the opportunity to play on his team! I played pickup ball with many of these women and the competition was always high.

During tryouts, Louis inquired about what university I graduated from. I didn't have an answer, so my response was, "Homeschool University." "I thought it was kinda funny, however, that did not go over well with Louis. It was at that moment that he set out to help me obtain my GED and then graduate from college. He saw that I was very talented and he refused to let my talents go to waste. Louis wasn't going to allow me to miss the opportunity to obtain an education, so he called up some coaches who he knew and drove me over 300 miles to play pickup basketball in an old gym in Lake Charles, Louisiana for a coach out of Mississippi.

Long story short, that year I received my GED and, my first of two basketball scholarships. I went on to play at Mississippi Gulf Coach Community College and upon graduation; I transferred to, and played, for The University of Memphis. It was there that I, earned a Bachelors in Kinesiology. It was because of people like Louis, who saw something greater in me that I was finally able to see greater things for myself. Because of his mentorship I became a first generation college graduate.

Upon my graduation from the University of Memphis, I continued to work out in hopes of getting an opportunity to play in the WNBA. That dream was shattered after I tore my ACL. This would be my fourth injury and I was 29 years old at the time. It just didn't make any sense to keep putting my body through such torment. My playing days were over. I became depressed and isolated myself from the game. I couldn't watch a game basketball without going through withdrawals. I felt like life was all but over for me. I wondered, what was I going to do now?

What was I going to do now?

It took me over a decade of transitioning from one career to another to figure it all out. **Transitioning out of sports into the "real world"** can be a confusing and painful time in an athlete's life. I had no clue what I was going to do next. I hadn't set up a Plan B.

What I didn't realize then, that I realize now is, there are attributes and transferable skills that we inherit as athletes that help us to master anything we set our minds to. Provided it's applied correctly.

Moreover, if you have been trained to work hard, to be a student of the game, to be motivated through your mistakes, to be resilient and persistent, and to have strong character, you can take those tools and apply them to any area of your life and emerge as a **champion** in that area. Sounds good! Right?

Not necessarily. It can be a catch-22 of sorts. When I transitioned out of sports I applied these principles to other careers. Even though I did not have the same passion as I did for basketball, I was able to excel fairy quickly. Eventually, I would become bored and sought out other opportunities to alleviate my boredom. As an athlete, I had a huge problem with being on the sidelines instead of in the midst of the game, therefore I had no desire to become a coach. That being said, I had no clue what I wanted to do after I could no longer play the game I loved. Then one day it came to me! Create content to help other transitioning athletes get out of their stumbling blocks and successfully transition into the next phase of their lives. It was that realization that caused CHAMPS U to be birthed. My flagship message, "Discover Your Inner Champion" focuses on the CHAMPS U model of taking the skills, gifts and talents you already possess and utilizing them in your personal and professional development. So here we are.

NCAA STATS

Men's Basketball

When we survey NCAA student-athletes, asking them about their expectations of moving on to professional athletics careers, the results indicate surprising confidence in that possibility. The reality is that very few go pro.

The estimated probability of competing in men's college basketball

High School Participants	NCAA Participants	Overall % HS to NCAA	% HS to NCAA Division I	% HS to NCAA Division II	% HS to NCAA Division III
541,479	18,697	3.5%	1.0%	1.0%	1.4%

Sources: High school figures from the 2014-15 High School Athletics Participation Survey conducted by the National Federation of State High School Associations. College numbers from the NCAA Sports Sponsorship and Participation Rates Report

The estimated probability of competing in men's professional basketball

NCAA Participants	Approximate # Draft Eligible	# Draft Slots	# NCAA Drafted	% NCAA to Major Pro*	% NCAA to Total Pro^
18,697	4,155	60	46	1.1%	12.2%

Women's Basketball

When we survey NCAA student-athletes, questioning them about their expectations of moving on to professional athletics careers, the results indicate surprising confidence in that possibility. The reality is that very few go pro.

The estimated probability of competing in women's college basketball athletics

High School Participants	NCAA Participants	Overall % HS to NCAA	% HS to NCAA Division I	% HS to NCAA Division II	% HS to NCAA Division III
429,504	16,589	3.9%	1.2%	1.1%	1.6%

Sources: High school figures from the 2014-15 High School Athletics Participation Survey conducted by the National Federation of State High School Associations. College numbers from the NCAA Sports Sponsorship and Participation Rates Report

The estimated probability of competing in women's professional basketball

NCAA Participants	Approximate # Draft Eligible	# Draft Slots	# NCAA Drafted	% NCAA to Major Pro*	% NCAA to Total Pro^
16,589	3,686	36	33	0.9%	

Football

When we survey NCAA student-athletes, questioning them about their expectations of moving on to professional athletics careers, the results indicate surprising confidence in that possibility. The reality is that very few go pro.

The estimated probability of competing in college football

High School Participants	NCAA Participants	Overall % HS to NCAA	% HS to NCAA Division I	% HS to NCAA Division II	% HS to NCAA Division III
1,083,617	72,788	6.7%	2.6%	1.8%	2.4%

Sources: High school figures from the 2014-15 High School Athletics Participation Survey conducted by the National Federation of State High School Associations. College numbers from the NCAA Sports Sponsorship and Participation Rates Report

The estimated probability of competing in professional football

NCAA Participants	Approximate # Draft Eligible	# Draft Slots	# NCAA Drafted	% NCAA to Major Pro*	% NCAA to Total Pro^
72,788	16,175	256	256	1.6%	1.9%

Baseball

When we survey NCAA student-athletes, inquiring about their expectations of moving on to professional athletics careers, the results indicate surprising confidence in that possibility. The reality is that very few go pro.

The estimated probability of competing in college baseball

High School Participants	NCAA Participants	Overall % HS to NCAA	% HS to NCAA Division I	% HS to NCAA Division II	% HS to NCAA Division III
486,567	34,198	7.0%	2.1%	2.2%	2.7%

Sources: High school figures from the 2014-15 High School Athletics Participation Survey conducted by the National Federation of State High School Associations. College numbers from the NCAA Sports Sponsorship and Participation Rates Report.

The estimated probability of competing in professional baseball

NCAA Participants	Approximate # Draft Eligible	# Draft Picks	# NCAA Drafted	% NCAA to Major Pro*	% NCAA to Total Pro^
34,198	7,600	1,215	738	9.7%	–

(http://www.ncaa.org/about/resources/research/probability-competing-beyond-high-school)

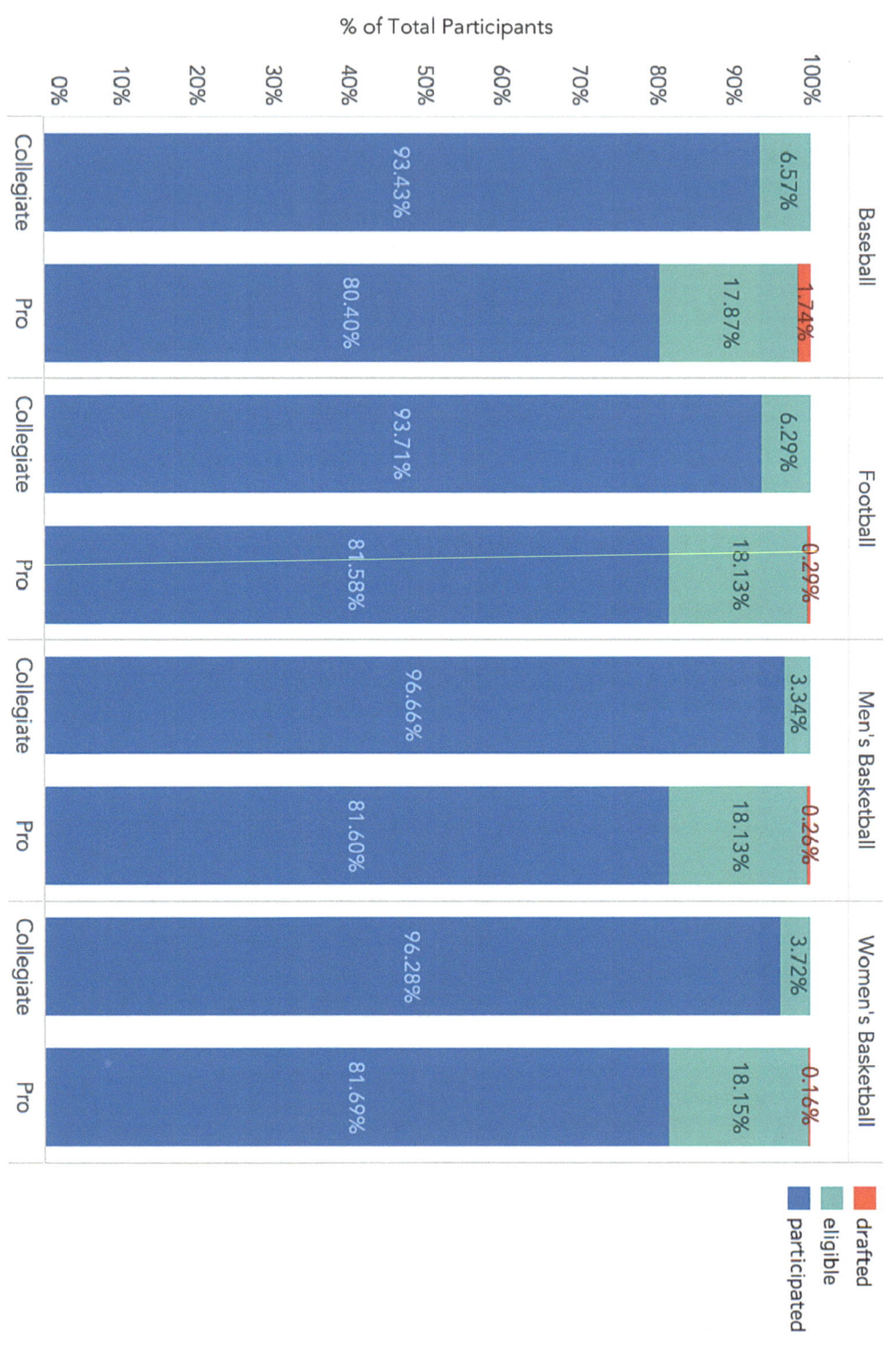

"Don't walk through life just playing football. Don't walk through life just being an athlete. Athletics will fade. Character and integrity and really making an impact on someone's life, that's the ultimate vision, that's the ultimate goal - bottom line."

-Ray Lewis

SECTION 1: MY MISSION

My mission, as an Athletepreneur (athlete turned entrepreneur) and coach, is to help student athletes like you to avoid the painful mistakes of not understanding or identifying your transferable skills, and how to implement those skills to create success around your strengths, passions and values, after your playing days are completed. I will help you identify your inner strength and teach you how to harness it to live a more focused, purposeful life as you transition from being a college athlete to living a successful life beyond the game. I consider my experience a cautionary tale.

In this guide we will do the following:

- Identify Athlete Identity
- Identify specific issues that affect student-athletes
- Gain clarity on how to move beyond sports and successfully transition into the professional world
- Learn how to formulate a success plan
- Learn how to create action steps that transition your dream into reality

CHAMPS U Principles of Success uses three core principles to support athletes in preparing for Championing success in sports, and in life after sports. These three core principles are as follows:

1. **CHAMPS characteristics of success (Personal Growth and Development)**
2. **MVP Mindset (Mindfulness and Awareness)**
3. **BRAND U (Professional Development)**

What Does CHAMPS (U) Stand for?

Coachable

Hunger for learning

Accountability

Mastering your Mindset

Persistence

Strength through Struggles

Brand **U**

Before we dive into the guide, here are some suggestions on how to use it to achieve the best outcome

1. Highlight, underline and make plenty of notes. The adage is true, "What you put into it is what you'll get out of it." The more you interact with the material, the more you'll gain.

2. Go easy on yourself. You may be starting this guide in a weakened position. You may be blaming yourself for making poor life decisions. You may be recovering from a career-ending injury and feel like life as you know it is over. You may be berating yourself for what you aren't doing, or for the mistakes you've made. That's o.k., welcome to the human race… We ALL make mistakes and things happen to us that are out of our control. We're going to spend time celebrating what you HAVE done right and then show you HOW to empower yourself in greater ways to successfully transition from collegiate sports and focus and celebrate your ah-ha moments and the progress you're sure to make.

3. Stay realistic. Being honest with yourself about where you are right now, and what you hope to accomplish, is key to creating enduring life successes. Unrealistic goals will not serve you well. You will learn to set attainable life goals that will challenge you and that are sustainable over the long haul.

4. Write down your thoughts. After answering the questions in each section, use the space provided to journal your thoughts, whether it is your doubts, challenges, insecurities, victories, and milestones. Whatever you are thinking, write it down. You'll be surprised at the progress you've made as you go back and read your entries.

Now, let's begin our journey to championing transition!

First things first

You must understand who you are before you know where you're going.

Who are you?

When asked the question, who are you, does your answer sound something like this;

"My name is _____ and I am a _____ (insert your sport or profession) at (school, company, etc.) _____."

Notice you just described **what** you do, and not **who** you are. Most people tend to get caught up in their (what I do) identity. In sports, this often happens to athletes who have participated in a specific sport starting at an early age. I started playing basketball at age seven, therefore until I transitioned out of actively participating in sports, when asked what I did I would say, I am:

- A basketball player
- A semi-pro player
- A collegiate basketball player
- A member of the University of Memphis Women's basketball team
- An athlete

And, I also know what it feels like to have a passion for playing a game, then having it ripped from your grips. I've felt lost and confused in my journey so I understand how crucial it is to **know who you are outside of sports.**

Who are you outside of sports?

We are multi-dimensional beings. Each of us has many roles/identities that we associate ourselves with. Look at the following list to see how many you identify with:

- ☐ Student
- ☐ Son/Daughter
- ☐ Friend
- ☐ Mentor
- ☐ Fashion lover
- ☐ Artist

- ☐ Sibling
- ☐ Girlfriend/Boyfriend
- ☐ Volunteer
- ☐ Avid music listener
- ☐ Photographer
- ☐ Writer

If you need to add your own here:

_____   _____

_____   _____

_____   _____

Get the picture? The list goes on and on.

Important definitions to remember:

What is Identity?

Who someone is: the qualities, beliefs, etc., that make that particular person or group different from others. *(Merriam-webster.com)*

What is Athletic Identity ?

The degree of importance, strength and exclusivity attached to the athletic role that is maintained by the athlete and influenced by their environment. *(Thomas J Cieslak II, M.A. 2004 p. 38)*

What is Identity Foreclosure?

Identity foreclosure is a stage of self-identity discovery in which an individual has an identity but hasn't explored other options or ideas. This is most common in young adolescents. In this stage, the individual has simply adopted the traits and qualities of parents and friends. *(alleydog.com)*

What is Transition?

defines Transition as the movement, passage, or change from one position, state, stage, subject, concept, etc., to another; change: (Example-the transition from adolescence to adulthood.) *(Dictionary.com)*

What is Athletic Transition?

The process of transitioning from actively participating or competing in sport. In order to progress beyond this stage a person must develop their own identity by questioning their own traits and exploring other options.

What makes student-athletes different from other students?

Student Athlete Stressors

Student-athletes face a plethora of daily stressors, both physically and emotionally. Besides the stressors they face in a classic college setting, student-athletes take on a heavier workload and have greater time obligations, adding to the impact. When they are no longer actively participating in sports there is now a void within their life, both mentally and physically.

Pressure to perform in both school and athletics, keeping a strong relationship with their coaches and maintaining a positive image with their fan base, both on and off the field challenge student athletes. Between practices, games, and school, athletes often don't have the luxury of additional time to have jobs in order to earn money for the things they need. This creates additional stress when it comes to buying food and other essentials necessary to exist. Once you're no longer playing your sport, these stressors become more intense, although your ability to get a job might increase. You might have been used to others providing for you but now it will be up to you to earn what you need in order to live.

Negative effects of athletic transitioning for collegiate competitors:

- Athletic Retirement: is defined as "the process of transition from participation in competitive sport to another activity or set of activities" (Coakley 1983, p. 1).
- Athletic Identity: is defined simply as "the degree to which an individual athlete identifies with the athlete role" (Brewer et al. 1993, p. 237).
- Several studies have shown that individuals who suffer from Athletic Identity are 'ill-equipped' when transitioning out of actively participating in sports. They also suffer from a higher rate of Identity Foreclosure. This experience can be life-altering, and in some severe cases, detrimental to the athletes' emotional and mental well-being.
- Schwenk et al. (2007) stated that the transition is often found to be difficult because of the sudden cessation of intense demands of elite athletic performance, compounded by the sudden loss of the athlete's intense devotion to professional athletic competition and its attendant rewards.
- Researchers have revealed that athletes may experience loss of appetite, weight fluctuation, insomnia, mood changes, a decline in motivation, depression, and lack of trust in others while going through sports retirement (Stankovich, Meeker & Henderson, 2001). Other researchers found that 42% of their respondents described a difficult sports retirement as *"quite characteristic"* or *"very characteristic"* (Webb, Nasco, Riley & Headrick, 1998).
- The next phase of life post-athletics can be quite challenging according to Jenny Moshak, ATC, who wrote "The Next Arena: Transitioning to Life after Collegiate Athletics." Ms. Moshak asserts, "Things that were planned (for her) as a student-athlete are now her responsibility – scheduling her day, eating nutritious meals, budgeting finances, carving out time to stay fit, building a new social and support structure, and finding new forms of exercise which for her includes yoga, hiking, and cycling."
- Sports career termination induces dramatic changes in athletes' personal, social and occupational lives; this can, in turn, potentially affect individuals cognitively, emotionally and behaviorally (Taylor & Ogilvie, 1994).

What's Your Plan? (Self-Assessment Questions)

When preparing for transitioning, it's crucial that you answer the following questions before you take any action. Write down your answers in the space provided. You may not have all of these things figured out. These questions are to assist you in self-assessing where you are and in beginning to create a plan for life after college.

1. What's my plan after college?

   _____

   _____

   _____

2. What do I have a passion for? (Example: I love helping children.)

   _____

   _____

   _____

3. What industry or business do I find interesting? What is it about that particular industry that I want to learn more about?

   _____

   _____

   _____

4. What is my **WHY,** and **WHY** does it matter? (Your WHY is what motivates you to choose the industry you have chosen.)

_____

_____

_____

5. Do I believe my view of myself affects my transition? (Why or Why not?)

_____

_____

_____

6. What skillset do I currently have that will help me in the next level of my career?

_____

_____

_____

7. How will the skills I've learned as an athlete be useful as I transition into my career?

_____

_____

_____

PERSONAL NOTES AND THOUGHTS JOURNAL

> "Weakness of attitude becomes a weakness of character."
>
> - Albert Einstein

SECTION 2: CHAMPS **(U)**-PRINCIPLES OF SUCCESS

Character plays a huge role in how successful you become and in your ability to maintain success. In this section, you will learn the CHAMPS characteristic for success. Here we have broken it down into an acronym to help you to remember them.

CHAMPS CHARACTERISTICS OF SUCCESS: These are the characteristics of a true champion. We all have areas in our lives that we would like to champion. These areas could be strengths that you want to make stronger or weaknesses that you want to shore up.

Through research and personal experience, I have been able to outline the practices and characteristics I have discovered that many champions in business, entrepreneurship, sports, and life utilize in order to stay ahead of the pack.

Let's explore the CHAMPS U Principles of Success!

(C)- COACHABLE

Be Coachable

To develop character one must be coachable and open to constructive criticism, corrections. They must always be seeking solutions versus constantly focusing on the problem. Character plays a huge role in how one will deal with the stressors of life. Seeking mentorship from someone who has been where you are hoping to go is one of the best methods you can adopt.

Be realistic in your answers below. Remember that these are tools for you to evaluate yourself and focus on areas that are relevant to you and only you. Circle the answer based on 1 being lowest and 10 being a highest. (Example: If you feel you are very coachable circle 10 if you are so, so circle 5.)

1. On a scale of 1 – 10, circle how open and receptive you are to constructive criticism, correction, and improvement suggestions:

1   2   3   4   5   6   7   8   9   10

    Low   High

2. If you didn't rate yourself at 10 for the previous question what steps can you take to get better?

_____

_____

_____

The Power of Mentorship

A great mentor is someone who is more knowledgeable than you, who positively impacts your personal and or professional growth, by sharing their knowledge. Being coachable is a very essential ingredient when it comes to mentorship. In the story I shared in the beginning of this guide, I spoke about my mentor, Louis Ray. He played a valuable role in helping me to focus on what was important in my life. In turn, I became a first generation college graduate. If he had not been in my life, I am not sure if I would have ever gone to college. Having a good mentor is priceless. You have the opportunity to learn without having to bump your head 100 times. Why step on the same land mines as those who have gone before you? A good mentor can also help motivate and inspire you to push yourself during challenging times. In order to benefit from a great mentor, you must be coachable. If I had not listened to Louis, I probably would not have gone to college. I didn't really see the benefit of having an education until he showed me.

1. Do you have a mentor? Circle one.

Yes   No

2. What qualities do you believe make a great mentor?

_____

_____

_____

3. If your answer to question #4 was no, how will you go about obtaining a mentor?

_____

_____

_____

4. Identify one area of improvement that would benefit your character and make you a better person. How do you think this will affect your preparation for transitioning out of college?

(Examples: Better time management, being more consistent, to stop procrastinating, eliminating excuses, being more coachable, etc.)

_____

_____

_____

5. If you answered No to question #1 - Who is in your current network that can possibly become your mentor?

_____

_____

_____

PERSONAL NOTES AND THOUGHTS JOURNAL

"Luck has nothing to do with my success. I have spent many, many hours, countless hours, on the court working for my one moment in time, not knowing when it would come."

-Serena Williams

(H)-HUNGER FOR LEARNING

Champions are always seeking to learn more

1. What are you passionate about outside actively participating in sports?
   _____
   _____
   _____

2. What industry do you want to learn more about? If it's the sports industry what job within sports do you want to learn more about?
   _____
   _____
   _____

Be a Student of the GAME (Research)

It's time to research the industries that align with your passions and interests. Be sure to study, participate, and develop your craft daily.

Tips on how to research your interests:
- Reading about the industry (books, research paper, etc.)
- Research articles and blogs that speak to your interests
- Listening to podcasts, TED Talks, etc.
- Attending seminars, lectures, and workshops

As a public speaker and coach, I studied speakers and coaches who aligned with my values, and who had already achieved the success I wanted to achieve.

I hired a speaking coach to assist me with my craft and a business coach to help me create a success plan.

I also attended conferences and workshops to help me with my stage presence and with properly preparing speeches.

-Who are the industry leaders in those careers, and who do you know that is in that field? Or, think of someone you know who knows someone in that field who can assist you. (Network, network, network…)

_____

_____

_____

For more information on coaching services visit (www.pashacook.com/CHAMPSU).

"Surround yourself with only people who are going to lift you higher."

-Oprah Winfrey

(A)-ACCOUNTABILITY

Merriam-Webster defines **Accountability** as, the quality or state of being accountable; especially**:** an obligation or willingness to accept responsibility or to account for one's actions.

1. **How to hold yourself accountable for your life:**
    a. Be honest with yourself about where you are and what you need.
    b. Give 100 % effort to every task.
    c. Set personal and professional goals.
    d. Focus on priorities by creating a weekly to-do list.
    e. Be open to asking for help.
    f. Surround yourself with others who will hold you accountable.

Building your Accountability Team

Accountability is the assignment of responsibility for outcomes to an individual or group to create an incentive for performance. Teams are accountable for achieving collective goals. Individual team members are accountable to each other for their effort and contributions to the team. (boundless.com)

Who is on your Accountability Team?

2. **An Ideal accountability team:**
    a) Has command goals
    b) Support each other
    c) Hold each other accountable for goals and ambitions
    d) Motivate each other to be and do better
    e) Demonstrate optimistic viewpoints
    f) Elevate each other to higher levels of thinking

Who can help me?

1. Who is in my current network that can help guide me through my athletic transition? Make a list of a few names. (**Friends, family, staff, career advisor, etc.?**)

   _____

   _____

   _____

2. What benefits does your current close network bring to you?

   _____

   _____

   _____

3. If you don't have an accountability team, list the names of people who you believe can speak with about being on your team.

   _____

   _____

   _____

4. How are you going to ensure that your accountability team has a united vision for your success? Do they share the same values?

   _____

   _____

Champion Action Steps:

1. Once you assemble your accountability team, describe to each member your expectations of them. Ask them what they expect from you.

2. If possible, have a regular weekly or monthly check-in with those on your team. Encourage them to openly share their ideas and any concerns or questions they have. (In the business world we call this "masterminding")

3. Write down your doubts and perceived challenges. You will do this for each of the CHAMPS U Principles. (By *perceived* challenges, I mean that the challenges we face often aren't really challenges at all; they just need a different perspective.) Seek help with working through list by sharing it with your mentor, counselor, accountability partner or someone your trust.

_____

_____

_____

Dictionary.com defines networking as, a supportive system of sharing information and services among individuals and groups having a common interest:

Networking is relationship building.

Networking resources:

There are some additional ways to build your team and meet people who can help you achieve your career goals. Consider the following:

Networking

- **Online platforms for networking**

LinkedIn

Instagram

Facebook

Twitter

Founder Dating

Athletenetwork.com

Or other social media platforms that include your peer group…

- **In-person platforms for networking**

Meetups

Conferences

Seminars

School events & groups, clubs, etc.

- **Utilize your current and past resources**

Stay connected with as many of your coaches, administrators, support staff, and as many other sports professionals as possible. Whether it is at the high school, collegiate, or professional level, networking is all about who you know and can get connect with.

Campus Resources: (check all that apply)

- ☐ teacher(s) ☐ administrator(s) ☐ other campus resources (groups)
- ☐ consultant(s) ☐ former athletes ☐ coaches
- ☐ career advisors ☐ community resources ☐ other alumni

Other _____

PERSONAL NOTES AND THOUGHTS JOURNAL

"Life is only as good as your mindset"

— Unknown

SECTION 3: (M)-Mastering Your Mindset

Did you know your mind is a muscle? It requires workouts and healthy regimens in order to grow stronger and to obtain peak performance, just like your body does.

In this section we will explore the mind muscle and how you can increase your awareness and mental game.

Susan Krauss Whitbourne Ph.D., in her article entitled, "Building a Better Brain: Strengthening your Mental Muscle", states, "Fortunately there are ways to build your mental muscle and give yourself that added boost. One way is through aerobic exercise, normally thought of as the antidote to premature cardiovascular disease.

The areas of the brain involved in attention and working memory seem to benefit from a workout that makes you sweat as much as does your heart. Watching what you eat can also help build your brain. Foods high in Omega-3, such as salmon, are truly "brain food." Even better, flavonoids, found in certain foods ranging from fruits and vegetables to red wine and dark chocolate, can also have a beneficial influence on cognition."

There is a multitude of ways to develop a workout regimen to strengthen your mental muscle; including free brain games like the Lumosity app, but perhaps building mental discipline is the most important. Tackling things, you hate to do FIRST and doing those tasks with maximum effort, helps to discipline your mind.

A daily routine of mindful meditation, visualization, and breathing will prepare your mind for the day's tasks. Kelly McGonigal Ph.D. instructor at Stanford University ranks meditation as the #1 way to increase willpower. She says, *"Practicing mindfulness meditation for a few minutes each day can actually boost willpower by building up gray matter in areas of the brain that regulate emotions and govern decision making."*

Resource: https://www.psychologytoday.com/blog/fulfillment-any-age/201004/building-better-brain-strengthening-your-mental-muscle

Recommended read- Carol Dweck's- "Mindset. *The physiology of success."*

(M)-MASTERING YOUR MINDSET: Why is it important to master our mindset? We are all creatures of habit. So, in order to create and maintain a champion's mindset, you will have to practice healthy mental habits. As athletes we are competitive, and no one wants to lose. We have been taught to work on our physical bodies in order to become stronger, faster and more physically prepared to compete with our opponents. If you have been a part of a successful program you have also had to work on your mental game. "Where the mind goes the body will flow."

MVP- Mindset Formula for Success:

1. Remain **M**otivated Thru **M**istakes. (Focus on the next play, not the last play)

You must be open to learning from your mistakes and not allowing the fear of making mistakes to paralyze your progress. Many people become fearful of making mistakes because they have identified mistakes as negative outcomes, instead of as opportunities to learn. Champions are motived by the challenges of making mistakes. They identify mistakes as areas of growth and are willing to learn from them and try it again.

   a. How do you typically handle mistakes and what emotions tend to surface when you make a mistake or error in judgment?

   _____

   _____

   _____

   b. Where do you see room for improvement? What steps can you take to improve?

   _____

   _____

   _____

2. Visualize your success. Visualizing your success is a way to increase success and decrease stress. Champions understand the power of visualization. Taking the time to mentally prepare for winning is just as important as physical practice. Below you will discover techniques that will help you gain clarity and focus.

    a. Are you currently practicing visualization? Circle your answer.

    Yes   No

    b. Think of one circumstance you're going through right now and write out what you're going to visualize as a positive outcome.

_____

_____

_____

Action Step: Carve out at least 15 minutes to practice visualizing positive outcomes. I recommend you do this in the morning before you start your day. This practices could also be utilized on game days, before interviews, and in any area of your life in which you would like to achieve success.

Step by step:

1. Get in a quiet and comfortable space where you will not be disturbed. (If you do not have a space in your dorm or apartment, some alternatives can be in the shower, in the library or outside on a park bench.)

2. Practice taking slow deep breaths, to relax you. Deep breathing has been shown to reduce stress.

3. As you relax, begin to visualize the area you would like to champion.

Example: seeing yourself making all your free-throws, shaving minutes off your qualifying time, passing your English exam etc.) How will it feel when you are able to champion this area? Hold on to that feeling throughout your day. This practice can be used for practically any area of your life. Be sure to focus on one area at a time.

3. Be **P**atient during the process

Patience is the state of mental endurance under difficult circumstances, which can mean persevering in the face of delay or provocation without acting on negative annoyance/anger; or exhibiting forbearance when under strain, especially when faced with longer-term difficulties. Patience is the level of mental endurance one can have before negativity. It is also used to refer to the character trait of being steadfast. *(Wikipedia.org/wiki/Patience)*

a. What areas of your life do you find yourself having a lack of patience?

_____

_____

_____

b. How can you begin to work on your patience?

_____

_____

_____

PERSONAL NOTES AND THOUGHTS JOURNAL

"What you are as a person is far more important than what you are as a basketball player."

- John Wooden

SECTION 4: (P)-PERSISTENCE

Choose one or more below that best describe you:

1. I want everything to happen NOW; no if's, and's, or but's about it!
2. I'm fairly patient with the process of transitioning and I'm hoping that it will all work out in the end.
3. I have NO patience at all! I'm going to do what I'm going to do and nobody will get in my way!
4. I'm willing to be patient with the transition process because doing things the right way will produce my desired results.

So, which of the four resonated with you?

#1? It's crucial to realize that all events happen exactly when they're supposed to happen and we cannot force the hands of time. We can prepare. We can set our vision. We can create our goals. But, we need to rest in the fact that our career and post-athlete life will unfold in layers. We don't want to rush to be ahead of events and we also don't want to lag behind either.

#2? It's good to hope for the best and to believe that it will all work out in the end. That doesn't mean you lean back, do nothing, and wait for all the pieces to magically fall into place.

#3? Like #1, there's a danger in pushing ahead recklessly just because you want your way and you want it NOW. You're headed for trouble if you fail to take a step back and assess your situation carefully and thoughtfully before moving.

#4? In a perfect world, everyone would be patient and do things the right way. But…we're not in a perfect world and impatience will show up occasionally. As you demonstrate patience with your transition process, set realistic goals, surround yourself with supportive people, and do things in a methodical way, not the fastest way, desired results will show up.

PERSONAL NOTES AND THOUGHTS JOURNAL

(P)-PERSISTENCE

Merriam-Webster defines Persistence as, "The quality that allows someone to continue doing something or trying to do something even though it is difficult or opposed by other people." The Urban Dictionary is much more succinct, by defining it as, "Unrelenting, someone who never gives up. Ceaseless." No matter where you go for your definition we all know that persistence is never giving up… period.

Persistence will help you do or achieve something regardless of any setbacks you might encounter along the way. The five things you must possess in order to exercise persistence are:

1) **Know exactly what your vision is.** The clearer it is, the more likely you are to achieve it.

2) **A burning desire to make it happen.** World-renowned motivational speaker, Jim Rohn, once said, *"If you really want to do something, you'll find a way. If you don't, you'll find an excuse."*

3) **Quiet confidence.** No need to shout in grandiose fashion to the world all you plan to do. Just know with inner-confidence that you will do it.

4) **A healthy dose of self-discipline.** Developing daily habits that support your vision is crucial as you continue down the path toward your goals.

5) **Be willing to change the game plan.** When a team is losing big, a good leader is not afraid to change the game plan in order to adapt to what the other team is doing. The persistent person sees their journey as a series of game plan tweaks, fouls, and timeouts. However, they still have complete faith they will reach their final destination.

1. Do you think you are a persistent person? Why or why not?

   _____

   _____

   _____

2. List three ways you can develop your persistence even further, especially when setbacks show up. (e.g Think before you react, be motivated by your mistakes, Etc.) You are not your mistakes, learn from them and keep moving forward.

   _____

   _____

   _____

3. From the five things you must possess to exercise persistence (read paragraph above once again). Which one do you consider a weaker point for you personally? Which one is the strongest?

   _____

   _____

   _____

"If you're not making mistakes, then you're not doing anything. I'm positive that a doer makes mistakes."

John Wooden

(S)-DEVELOP STRENGTH THROUGH YOUR STRUGGLES

Muscle building cannot occur without first tearing down muscle fibers. Hypertrophy is the term used to describe an increase in muscle bulk, which occurs when the body repairs torn muscle fiber. This process occurs during heavy weightlifting. It is not a comfortable process; however, it is necessary in order to build strength. Hear me clearly when I say, "There is no growth in your comfort zone."

The good news is; you can stop looking at your struggles as negative. You can stop concluding that your failures are final. Struggles are the coal that fuels the fire of your character. Struggles build muscle in your inner-self so even though they're not pleasant to go through, they do serve a greater purpose.

As I stated, your failures are not final. They do not define who you are nor who you will become. Every great man or woman has experienced failure, often multiple times. If you've failed at something, that simply means you were trying. You weren't sitting passively; you were in action. John Maxwell, in his book, "Failing Forward," says, "The difference between average people and achieving people is their perception of and response to failure."

I combat negativity and build myself up mentally by listening to motivational YouTube videos, reading 20-30 pages of something positive and setting positive intentions daily, within the first 20 minutes after I awake. It helps me to start my day on an upbeat note.

Don't overthink and over-analyze your situation. Picking a situation apart over and over causes negative thoughts. That is NOT how you want to spend your precious time. Stop over-thinking and just go do what's on your list. Learn from the experience and keep moving forward.

1. Describe a major struggle that has caused you to grow stronger mentally and emotionally.

   _____

   _____

   _____

2. What are the major strengths you have gained through the struggle?

   _____

   _____

   _____

3. What is your plan to power through future struggles and failures, both large and small?

   _____

   _____

   _____

4. What would you tell a friend who is struggling with a life challenge? *(Note: We are often more compassionate towards others than we are towards ourselves. Whatever loving expression you would use towards your friend is the same words you need to use towards yourself during your times of struggle.)*

   _____

   _____

   _____

5. List five of your strengths below.

_____

_____

_____

6. Ask 3 people (Accountability partner, mentor, coach, family member, etc.) to provide feedback on the strengths you've listed.

_____

_____

_____

PERSONAL NOTES AND THOUGHTS JOURNAL

"Your brand is what other people say about you when you're not in the room."

- Jeff Bezos, CEO of Amazon

SECTION 5: BRAND **(U)**

In this section, you will learn how to build your personal brand.

In a world that teaches us to share our lives in front of thousands of strangers, it is very competitive and more difficult than ever to stand out in the crowded world of the internet.

In today's marketplace of technology and innovation, how we brand ourselves has become a huge part of how successful we are. From obtaining jobs, business partnerships and building online relationships, long gone are the days when all you had to do was graduate from college with good grades or write a stellar resume.

You must understand that YOU are a brand and you are living this brand each and every day. Resumes require keywords and employers have teams of people who research you via the internet to get an idea of who you are and what you are doing. If you have a LinkedIn profile you have the option of seeing everyone who views your page. You would be surprised at some of the people who will check you out online after having a short conversation with you at the local Starbucks.

- 94% of recruiters are using LinkedIn to discover talent.
- 65% are using Facebook
- 55% are on Twitter.

Personal Branding and how using technology can help

SOCIAL MEDIA AWARENESS is crucial to brand development

(Instagram, Twitter, Snapchat, LinkedIn, Facebook)

Postings on any social media are forever (there are no do-overs). Everything you post, respond or react to is for all of the world to see.

Personal Branding and Social Media

What's your personal brand?

- When I refer to you as being a "brand" what I mean is that you are the public persona you put out into the world. It's how you become known to others.

- In order to understand how to brand yourself, you first need to identify your values, the values you bring and your strengths. I recommend you working through this section with your advisor, counselor, accountability partner or mentor for the feedback questions.

What are your values?

- An excellent way to figure out what makes you happy is by identifying your values. By understanding your values, you will be able to gain clarity in which direction you wish to go after college, you will decrease stress, and this will help you to create a roadmap for your success action steps.

- By participating in this assessment you will identify your top values, and assess whether you are presently aligned with those values.

- When I started my company I wanted to work in a field that supported the **competitiveness** of my sports background, one that allowed me to travel, and that also provided me the **flexibility** to spend time with my friends and **family**.

Use the table on the next page to complete this exercise.

Step 1 –Highlight the five words that resonate with you. If you don't see the word(s) that best describes your current values, feel free to add them at the bottom of the worksheet.

Step 2 – Now narrow the list to your top three by crossing out two of your choices.

Step 3 – Finally put a circle on the one value that most resonates for you.

Advancement	Commitment	Health	Caring	Generosity
Fame	Kindness	Respect	Humor	Discipline
Celebrity	Affluence	Health	Growth	Peace
Teamwork	Vision	Wealth	Spontaneity	Independence
Adventure	Creativity	Higher Purpose	Family	Faith
Resourcefulness	Economic Security	Pleasure	Power	Balance
Flexibility	Comfort	Adventure	Control	Generosity
Aesthetics	Cultural Awareness	Lifelong learning	Relationships	Recognition
Authenticity	Excellence	Resilience	Stability	Challenge
Love	Loyalty	Justice	Ambition	Security
Autonomy	Fairness	Honesty	Perfection	Spirituality

Self-Reflection Questions:

1. What value matters most to you? What does this value mean to you (how do you define it)?

_____

_____

_____

2. Why do your top 3 values or beliefs stand out above all the others for you?

_____

_____

_____

3. Are you currently living these values in your life?

_____

_____

_____

4. How can you start to live these values more in your life?

_____

_____

_____

5. How do you want the world to perceive you? When people see your name, what's the first thing you want them to think of?

_____

_____

_____

6. What do you want potential employees, clients or business associates to see when they search for you on the internet?

_____

_____

_____

7. What value do you bring? List your natural talents, transferable skills and strengths.

_____

_____

_____

8. What is your vision for yourself after college?

_____

_____

_____

9. What do you feel makes your brand unique? Why?

_____

_____

_____

CHAMPS (U) Success Action Steps:

Write a short plan on how you'll develop clarity and vision for your brand. Include how you plan to maintain your brand and transition it to the next level in order to keep it current and relevant. (Your plan will develop and change over time. Do your research and gradually begin to layout your blueprint for success.)

_____

_____

_____

_____

_____

_____

_____

_____

_____

_____

_____

_____

_____

GUIDE SUMMARY

List your **top** five takeaways from this guide.

1. _____

2. _____

3. _____

4. _____

5. _____

CHAMPS WORKBOOK

Based on what you learned from the guide, answer the following questions:

1. Visualize yourself three years from now. How has your network grown and developed? What type of people are in your inner-circle? Who are you helping and who is helping you?

   _____

   _____

   _____

2. Visualize your perfect day once your transition is fully complete and write about it. Use all your senses. Include as many concrete details as you can. Are you working from home, an office, or a collaborative workspace? What items surround you, e.g.: candles, air fresheners, books, etc.? What's on your desk? What time do you start your day and end your day? Do you go to the gym before or after you start work? Are you the boss, an employee, or entrepreneur?

   _____

   _____

   _____

3. What will be your plan for maintaining a healthy mind, body, and spirit? How will you continue getting regular exercise, and enough sleep when you are no longer an college athlete? What will be your daily practices?

   _____

   _____

   _____

4. How will you maintain stability in your life so you don't get out of balance in any one area?

_____

_____

_____

5. How will you spend your down time? And, yes, even in the midst of transition, you need recreational time. Will you read? Write? Travel? Attend local festivals? Learn a new language?

_____

_____

_____

6. Have your doubts and perceived challenges changed during completing this guide? Take a moment and explain any shifts in mindset.

_____

_____

_____

Champion Action Steps:

1. Using the CHAMPS U acronym, list two actions for each principle that you will implement over the next 30 days. Start your sentence with "I will…" Remember to be patient with yourself.

1. Character

1. _____

2. _____

2. Hunger for Learning

1. _____

2. _____

3. Accountability

1. _____

2. _____

4. Mastering Your Mindset

1. _____

2. _____

5. Persistence

1. _____

2. _____

6. Strength Through Your Struggles

1. _____

2. _____

Congratulations! You've completed this guide. Review it often to stay on track and to make notes of any new ideas or thoughts that come to mind. Record any setbacks you experience along the way, including how you reacted to them, and how you can do better next time. Learning how to Champion Athletic Transition will help you through every transition that life has to offer.

I practice the principles contained in this guide every day! I live by them and I've achieved more than I ever thought possible through the CHAMPS U concept. When I think back on the struggles I've endured and the road I've traveled, I'm so thankful that I discovered these principles and practices. They changed my life, and they can change yours too! The transition isn't easy but it's worth every minute you spend in the tunnel of transition. As you embrace and journey through your own transition from athletics into an exciting, abundant life, you will come out on the other side, stronger, happier, and better equipped to succeed and achieve anything you set out to do.

PERSONAL NOTES AND THOUGHTS

PERSONAL NOTES AND THOUGHTS

About the Author

Pasha Cook, a native of Houston, Texas, is a former collegiate standout. She earned a Bachelor of Science degree in Kinesiology from the University of Memphis in 2002; then she was propelled into identifying and drawing from a new strength. She combined her passion as an educator, experience as an entrepreneur, and love for sports to create an organization to meet a world-wide need for assisting athletes in creating a much better life beyond the game.

She utilizes more than a decade of experience in branding, image consulting and career development to help athletes in creating their unique brand, personal messaging and stories to effectively reach their target audiences (future employer, customer base, schools, etc.). She uses a variety of strategies to meet the unique needs of each athlete through her facilitation of transition workshops, leadership development training, and character building seminars.

As a forerunner of empowerment, Cook emphasizes the need for career development, branding, and marketing to engage athletes.

Cook partners with non-profit organizations, corporate sports organizations, and collegiate institutions to create seminars and forums that focus on the challenges predominantly associated with race, ethnicity, socio-economic status, and socio-culture background.

Her book is a must-read for the beginning athlete, the elite competitor, and the transitioning athlete. Her perspective is from someone who knows—someone who shares the perspectives that only an athlete has experienced. Her message is one of great expectation, newfound confidence, sustained hope, and fervent belief in a better life after the cheers from the crowd has ended.

For more information on Champs U please visit *(www.pashacook.com/champsu)*

Works Cited

Brewer, Britton W., et al. "Athletic Identity: Hercules' Muscles or Achilles Heel." *International Journal of Sport Psychology*, vol. 24, no. 2, 1993, pp. 237-54, psycnet.apa.org/psycinfo/1994-03969-001. Accessed 9 Nov. 2016.

Cieslak, Thomas J. *Describing and Measuring the Athletic Identity Construct: Scale Development and Validation*. Dissertation, Ohio State University, 2004.

Coakley, Jay J. "Leaving Competitive Sport: Retirement or Rebirth?" *Quest*, vol. 35, no. 1, 1983, pp. 1-11. *Taylor and Francis Online*, doi: dx.doi.org/10.1080/00336297.1983.10483777.

"Identity." *Merriam-Webster.com*. 9 Nov. 2016.www.merriam-webster.com/dictionary/identity utm_campaign =sd&utm_medium=serp&utm_source=jsonld.

"Identity Foreclosure." *Alleydog*, www.alleydog.com/glossary/definition-cit.php?term=Identity Foreclosure. Accessed 8 November 2016.

Krauss Whitbourne, Susan. "Building a Better Brain: Strengthening Your Mental Muscle." *Psychology Today*, 6 April 2010, www.psychologytoday.com/blog/fulfillment-any-age/201004/building-better-brain-strengthening-your-mental-muscle. Accessed 9 Nov. 2016.

McGonigal, Kelly. "Meditate Your Way to More Willpower: Meditation MP3s to Strengthen Self-Control and Self-Compassion." *Psychology Today*, 28 April 2010, www.psychologytoday.com/blog/the-science-willpower/201004/meditate-your-way-more-willpower. Accessed 9 Nov. 2016.

Moshak, Jenny. "The Next Arena: Transitioning to Life After Collegiate Athletics." *NCAA*, 2013, www.ncaa.org/health-and-safety/nutrition-and-performance/next-arena-transitioning-life-after-collegiate-athletics. Accessed 9 November 2016.

NCAA. "Probability of Competing Beyond High School." NCAA.org. N.p., 11 July 2016. Web. 08 Nov. 2016.

Schwenk, T.L., et al. "Depression and Pain in Retired Professional Football Players." *Medicine & Science in Sports & Exercise*, vol. 39, no. 4, 2007, pp. 599-605. *Wolters Kluwer*, doi: 10.1249/mss.0b013e31802fa679.

Shiina, S., et al. "Effects of Transferable Skills Workshops on the Career Self-Efficacy of College Student-Athletes." *Academic Athletic Journal*, vol. 17, no. 1, 2003, pp. 54-64.

Stankovich, C. E., et al. "The Positive Transitions Model for Sport Retirement." *Journal of College Counseling*, vol. 4, no. 1, 2001, pp. 81–84. *Wiley Online Library*, doi:10.1002/j.2161-1882.2001.tb00186.x. Accessed 9 Nov. 2016.

Taylor, J. & B.C. Ogilvie. "A Conceptual Model of Adaptation to Retirement Among Athletes." *Journal of Applied Sport Psychology*, vol. 6, no. 1, 1994, pp. 1-20. *Taylor and Francis Online*, doi: 10.1080/10413209408406462.

"Transition." *Dictionary.com Unabridged*. 9 Nov. 2016. www.dictionary.com/browse/transition.

Webb, W.M., et al. "Athlete Identity and Reactions to Retirement from Sports." *Journal of Sport Behavior*, vol. 21, no. 3, 1998, pp. 338–62, www.cabdirect.org/cabdirect/abstract/19981810694.

www.ingramcontent.com/pod-product-compliance
Lightning Source LLC
Chambersburg PA
CBHW042002150426
43194CB00002B/94